MAGNIFICENT MANSIONS

MAGNIFICENT MANSIONS

Matt Louis McCullough

Copyright © 2020 Matt Louis McCullough

All rights reserved.

ISBN-13: 9798648182554

Unless otherwise indicated, Scripture quotations are taken from the (NASB®) New American Standard Bible®, Copyright © 1960, 1971, 1977, 1995 by The Lockman Foundation. Used by permission. All rights reserved. www.Lockman.org

Scripture quotations noted KJV are from the King James Version of the Bible.

Table of Contents

Preface	VII
Acknowledgments	XI
CHAPTER ONE	
The Road More Traveled	1
CHAPTER TWO	
The Road Less Traveled	27
CHAPTER THREE	
"Monster Wrastle"	47
CHAPTER FOUR	
The Father's Mansion	55
CHAPTER FIVE	
Preparing a Place	65
CHAPTER SIX	
The Revealing	77
CHAPTER SEVEN	
The Final Leg	97

Preface

Each of our lives plays out as an allegory of something, though we may struggle to comprehend what that is. In any case, we are fortunate to play at all. We carry about in the flesh as a wonderfully made product of God's creation in a literal and tangible way. But being human, a living soul, is another matter altogether. Our being here is not just about the dust or clay we come from, a remarkable result of the material, but meaning, an eternal substance. We prefer to get out of the muck and make it to some higher ground. And we try.

So I begin the story somewhat on that notion. Yet, the narrative then alludes to the stark commonness of apparently unfulfilled lives. I proceed with my account of having had the hopeless feeling of being stuck, meaninglessly slogging about for decades without any sense of specific direction or calling. I have despaired over the thought of having wasted my life. Perhaps others are exhausted and disparaged in trying to escape the lowlands. Or worse, you have been dragged off of your nicely planned path, severely beaten down, and left beside the road. Maybe you feel you have already returned to the dust and may as well stay there. But I believe God will come through for you. He does for all of His children. After all, He did for me. And I am moved to share that message. Thus, *Magnificent Mansions* is a true story that offers encouragement and hope for seemingly failed and unfulfilled lives. It provides glimpses of God preparing a more glorious life than we can imagine, a mansion for us, even out of our dust.

This book presents a story. But it also works its way into a discussion. The discourse will challenge some "Christian" dogmas that I believe may unnecessarily lead to much frustration and disappointment. I also felt driven to share where and how elements of the message were derived.

Some came by way of a dreary wasteland of concrete. Bits more were noted within the grand theaters of our Lord's creation. And much of it occurred in the dead of night. But the theme of all of it came from hearing God's transformative words as found in the Scripture and by catching glimpses of Him expressed through others, in small exchanges, and unexpected ways. Many of my thoughts or experiences were written down at or near the moments they happened. So at times, you may have a real-time sense of the progression and a bit of mystery.

I also believe many of the events, concerns I had, and situations I was going through are widely relatable. And oddly, these literal happenings all seem connected and play out as some peculiar parable. But if one gets the impression this book is about me, my writing has failed miserably. The message intends for one to look at God, His work in us and through us. All of this is about the magnificent place He prepares for us. One we can come home to and rest. There, we have our lives fulfilled as we glorify Christ and are glorified with Him together. And that place may not be what you think.

Matt L. McCullough
December 13, 2020

Acknowledgments

Despite my skeptical brain, I am pretty sure I got to this point because God dealt with me. So by His peculiar manner, I felt motivated to write and share this book. Furthermore, Christ's expression of Himself and His splendid work, as I have seen in my family, friends, and others, were amply provided to make several of the main points.

Deep water to draw from came especially from my wife Carmen, kids Sarah and Andy, parents Weldon and Delores, sister Mickey, and brother-in-law Ray. My mom allowed me to share freely about events recorded in her unpublished manuscript detailing the life of her father, Louis Canada - a.k.a. "Shorty," and her mother, Betty. And I am grateful for Brian Chronister. He is the Anchorage pastor I refer to in the first chapter. A more adequate acknowledgment is given to him there. But I will add here that I had benefited much from his expository reading of the Bible and gift of teaching. Through Brian, I believe God drew my attention to the words of Scripture more than ever before. This, in turn, led me to intently read, question, and try and understand the context and meaning of them myself. Brian also gave me some useful and much-needed objective suggestions upon a brief review of my initial draft. Helpful and uplifting feedback also came from my dear friends Steve Taylor, Brent Neal, Huey Tang, Tricia Zody, and my sister-in-law Becky Weber.

But ultimately, if there is any good that comes from this writing, it would only be by God's doing nevertheless. So by every reckoning, thanks and honor are foremost given to Him. And I thank Him for those of you who would read this book. Perhaps through its words, you will find comfort when things do not altogether turn out the way you had hoped. May you find new hope and receive a glimpse now of the mansion Jesus is building for you too!

CHAPTER ONE

The Road More Traveled

We search and hope for a higher calling, to live more nobly, and to dwell in a grander manner and place. But some lives, even lived at their best, seem to die by sheer exhaustion and are left lying beside the dim roadside without reaching their desired destination. And others just waste away in the night waiting, or slowly while moving aimlessly along the dull plains. We plead in the night for comfort, understanding, and a little direction. While all along, we are haunted by the thoughts of the dead carcasses of our failed dreams and lives. But, often, we receive neither relief nor any sense of anything. Then, sometimes in the darkness, a mere glimmer, a small diffraction of light, comes through just enough to see not all that are dead have decayed in vain. We get a glimpse that their true elements are for the eons, an eternal body, and a nobler place after all. The darkness always yields to the light when there is any light at all — easily. So we long for and wait for illumination. To be able to start our ascent out of the lowlands with a good view of our purpose. And upward toward that higher ground and a grander place out there somewhere . . . sometime. But for me, that wait has been at least half of my life so far. And the years seemingly wasted and miles tread have been tiresome, especially in Houston, Texas. In that long haul, I hope only paradigms were lost, but not paradise. There must be that better place I seek, though I suspect it will be a little different from what I have imagined.

Just about anywhere within the Houston area, one hears the drone of car and truck traffic from a highway. It is one thing to have to listen to it continuously; it is another to drive, or more like crawl, along its roads for over two decades. I commuted to work from Sugar Land, a suburb on the southwest side of Houston. I recall the long twenty-mile slog too readily. Thousands of us would jostle about to continue forward down a freeway along a drab flatland of concrete, strip malls, strip clubs, franchise restaurants, mattress stores, car dealerships, and assorted highway debris. Inevitably, a day came that the oil company I worked at began to lay off the workers. And jobs like mine interpreting where oil and gas resources may be deep below the ocean floor were being cut.

Seeing an opportunity for a generous severance package, I asked to be let go at the end of my project assignment. The management accepted my offer. Three months later, I was very unclear about what to do next with my life. I had hoped to figure that out before then, but as I could have guessed, that did not happen. My last day of work was Friday, December 30, 2016. My boss and colleagues were off, and most of them had been gone a long while for the holidays. I decided to work most of that time to max-out my carry-over vacation pay into the time after my retirement. The hallways were dark, except for the light shining through to the portion by my office, and very quiet. I did not have much to do except clean my office and archive my digital work files in the proper computer folders. I usually could find someone to go with me to the lounge for a cup of coffee, but not that day. As I finished my last day of work at the company I had been with for over twenty-six years, I cleared my desk, turned off the computer, and turned the lights out. I then made my long way home.

When I was seventeen, I promised myself to live life to the fullest and pursue an exciting, adventurous, and meaningful career. My parents told me to seek God's will in the matter. I am sure I did or at least made some request to Him. But I did not have a clue how He would direct or lead me. All I knew at the time was that I liked the idea of being a marine biologist. I wanted to be like Jacques Cousteau and swim with whales and discover unknown worlds beneath the waves. After my first semester at a marine-science college and a little research, I realized jobs were scarce for marine biologists. One is more likely to end up studying the effects of a toxin in shellfish in a shallow bay *(borrring!)* than exploring the ocean. However, opportunities at the time were numerous for geologists in the petroleum industry. And geology was another interest of mine. At least geology included studying the earth beneath the ocean. So I pursued that course.

But as a young man, I would not have guessed I would settle for spending most of my adult working life at a large corporation sitting at an office desk most of the day, and wasting a lot of time . . . way too much time, while oddly making money at it. I tried to make the best of my career and was very grateful for the employment and a company that treated me well. I also got to collaborate, learn from, and work with a great bunch of people, and field trips as part of my training a couple of weeks a year took me to many countries around the world. But building quality relationships with colleagues was difficult since people frequently left the company or were moved around. And the work required me to be at a desk most of the time within a private office. However, the most frustrating aspect was the projects were often not carried out, even after working on them for years. And those implemented were usually of such a low chance of success that the outcome inevitably would be disappointing. Most of my work did not seem to contribute much or be meaningful in any way. The management appeared to make allowances for most of us involved with canceled projects or endeavors that fell short as long as we put in the effort. I am not sure how I passed that test. Except for clicking a computer mouse, I spent most of my time just thinking as I sat at my desk. The problem with thinking, though, is that it does not look like work. Yet, I was somehow able to stay employed. I often thought maybe it would be good if I got laid off and forced to take a different route with my life. But being married with two children to raise and having the professional level of pay that came with the position, I readily rationalized the need to keep my job. I was incredibly privileged to have that type of employment. Yet, I felt I had wasted most of my life. And with every mile I slogged down that freeway, I threw away more.

Along Houston roadsides, I would sometimes see billboards standing out above the lackluster terrain and lit up with pictures of beautiful destinations. They would remind me of a place in my far distant past. Days when I once felt led to a more productive ground than the stripped barren plains in which I have vainly traipsed. I was thinking back to when I was single in my early thirties. I got a reprieve from working in Houston by accepting a job transfer to Anchorage, Alaska.

The state intrigued me with its incredible beauty, but I had been a little hesitant to go because I had heard of a shortage of women there. I figured I was ready to be or should have been married by that time. Surprisingly, not too long after arriving there, I met and fell in love with a young woman in her early twenties. I chose to love and pursue her with everything I had. But after almost a year into our relationship, I felt in my gut something was not right. Despite some encouraging words she expressed, my perceptions of her behavior began to erode my confidence about marrying her. She seemed to enjoy maintaining a free spirit of a sort, and I felt I needed to give her more space. After a brief discussion with her one evening, I realized there was a significant distance between us and think I said something like, "So that's it?" Without many words exchanged, I gathered that she agreed. We stopped being with each other. A few weeks later, I was sitting alone one night in a dark movie theater when I saw her behind me with a new boyfriend. I slumped down in my seat so she would not see me by myself. She appeared to have moved on. However, I was still grieving over the separation and loss of my hope for our life together and perhaps every painful breakup I ever had.

As therapy for my loneliness, I would often pick out one of the women from my failed relationships and fantasize about her. But my choice usually involved one who discarded me in one way or another, hence deeming me an undesirable mate. Except, in my vainglorious daydreams, I was always the right guy for her. But she could not see it. Later, I would save her somehow. Whether rescuing her from a deadbeat boyfriend or being taken hostage by a savage tribe, it always involved my heroic courage or sacrifice. If only she had known, she would not have treated me so cold. I know that sounds a lot like one of those stories told so often in great books and movies and grabs your heart every time. One where there is a cloaked superhero, a huge misunderstanding, and then the revealing of the grandest sacrifice and love the world has ever known. In real life, though, I was not expecting anything like that, except for the misunderstandings. There are always those. And I would not likely experience even the least of my grandiose fantasies, which also contained more lustful thoughts than I care to admit. In any case, I knew to take such notions down a notch as a practical matter. I am not a hero, nor have I demonstrated a likely willingness to save someone while risking a significant chance of getting speared. I could maybe do the dishes, though. At least I had my imaginings left. Perhaps I had been more in love with an idea than any real person. I wasn't sure who or what I wanted. I only knew I was very lonely.

I found myself languishing in movie theaters, restaurants, and bars alone, especially during those dark Alaska days of winter far too often. I had not attended a church service in years, but someone happened to mention a "non-denominational church" I should go to that was not too condemning. In my mind, it must have come across as, "People like you will feel comfortable there." Though I did not necessarily think the rut I was stuck in was that bad, I decided for some reason to try a small change in my routine. I started to attend the services. And for over a year, the pastor, named Brian, taught from the book of Romans. Verse by verse, he read, expounded upon, and explained hard to understand portions of the writings. Much of the book was familiar, but this was the first time I began to understand something about God's grace. Enough so, to ease some lingering doubts I had from the sloppy faith of my past. And I did feel comfortable there listening to the words spoken by the pastor . . . or more like hearing the Word, more than I could ever remember.

To explain, let me wind even further back to my "theological beginnings." I am pretty sure I was like many young kids who attended a First Baptist Church, or similar ilk, with their parents. "Going down front" or "walking the aisle" was what one did as soon as your fear of taking that walk was less than burning in hell forever. As best as I understood, openly professing my faith in Jesus by walking down the aisle to the front of the congregation during the pastor's invitation was necessary for getting into heaven. At ten years old, I took that walk. But a few years later, I was asked, "Do you know that you know that you know that if you were to die tonight, that you would go to heaven?" It seems like that question came up every time I went to a revival service or a church youth camp. Well, I did not know that I knew. I thought back about my earlier profession of faith. I had little faith in my faith. And much less confidence in what was going on in the head of a ten-year-old.

You may be wondering, did I repent asking for forgiveness of my sin? Did I confess with my mouth and sincerely accept Jesus as my Lord and Savior? Did I believe in my heart that God raised Him from the dead? Though I am not a big fan of that stereotypical line of questioning, I will answer that. Yes, yes, and yes to the best I knew how. If I prayed the "Sinner's Prayer" once, I must have prayed it a hundred times. I can't recall ever not praying it. The pastor would lead that prayer in every service, and I don't see how one keeps from praying that prayer in his or her head, especially with that dying tonight part. Sincerely with all my heart, I wanted to get to heaven rather than the other fate. What kid would not want that? I'm sure I missed some critical elements of the preaching. But to avoid hindering children from actually coming to Jesus by way of their trust in Him, you would think one would not use fear so much as a motivator. Kids have enough anxieties already.

I could tell a much longer story about those early days of my so-called coming to Christ. But let it suffice to say, many years were spent worrying if I was really saved. And piled on top of that, it seemed like every sermon was about something I should have done or should be doing if I was a

"Christian." I needed to be obedient, let go, serve, commit, tithe, pray more, stop this, not do that, confess, pledge, support the mission, invite, and . . . you name it. Did I have enough faith, and was I doing enough to convince myself I was a real believer? It was as if it was all about me. Doubts about my salvation continued.

Fast forward now, that is, getting back again, to when I was in Anchorage. As I said, I had read a fair chunk of the book of Romans. And I am pretty sure I had listened to many sermons and was familiar with scriptures, some from the other letters of the apostle Paul, about grace. But for some reason, God dealt with me at this time through that pastor in Alaska. I began to hear about grace and its relation to my faith in a whole new way. Before, I had mostly understood what Paul meant when he wrote, "For by grace you have been saved through faith; and that not of yourselves, *it is* the gift of God; not as a result of works" (Eph. 2:8–9). I understood my salvation was not about works, but that "through faith" part had always stared me in the face and bothered me. If I am saved by grace through faith, then both appear to be critical to support my salvation. So if my faith must bear part of the load, how much faith is enough? To uphold my salvation, I was placing His grace as one pillar and my faith as another. But does the verse suggest that grace and faith must carry the same weight? After all, the words "by" and "through" are close in meaning. The moment I, my faith, was put anywhere into the equation, I tended to have doubts. But Christ systematically through Paul, through pastor Brian, and while I gazed intently at the black letters on a white page as I read along in the book of Romans, apparently dismantled my misguided reasoning.

There is not just one particular verse or chapter I could point to, but "faith *comes* from hearing, and hearing by the word of Christ" seems to sum up my experience pretty well (Rom. 10:17). It was not like I was choosing to hear, but by the words, His words,

He was drawing me to hear. I would have had to put in some effort to ignore Him. As verses came up about faith and grace, I began to focus intently on the words. For example, Paul stated, "Having been justified by faith, we have peace with God through our Lord Jesus Christ, through whom also we have obtained our introduction by faith into this grace in which we stand" (Rom. 5:1–2). I noticed that we are justified by faith, but Jesus is "through whom" we have access by faith to God's grace. I felt some burden begin to lift. And then I also caught the ending. It is "this grace in which we stand." I found I do not need to have faith in my faith. I only need to rely on His grace and accept that it is on this grace that I and my salvation stand as opposed to anywhere else. His grace, which we have through His provision, who is Christ, is sufficient. As if some doubt could still be lingering, Paul thoughtfully added, "For if while we were enemies we were reconciled to God through the death of His Son, much more, having been reconciled, we shall be saved by His life" (Rom. 5:10). Then I can most certainly rest securely on that kind of grace. Many more verses had drawn my attention as well, too numerous to mention. But the shift of load had begun to occur, and then I found I could completely rest. There was nothing needed by my effort to support, only one mighty pillar of grace. I merely accepted that I could stand there on it. And I have lain down and rested on it from pure exhaustion. And even that rest, I am pretty sure, is due to His grace.

It finally sunk into my fat noggin that God has done and does all that saving kind of work, including getting me to the point of accepting His offer. John the Baptist said, "A man can receive nothing unless it has been given him from heaven" (John 3:27). I realized my sins are forgiven because of God's grace and His provision and not because of anything I did or needed to do. And by recognizing I was truly free, this freed me to love Jesus. My desire grew to get to know about Him more, especially the one who had forgiven me so much. I started to read the Bible nightly with particular attention to the words of Jesus and what His disciples said about Him. My loneliness, inexplicably, started to melt away. I also began to see the wisdom in those words and get a sense of God's way of doing things that I had not realized before. I wanted to put God first and even told Him in a prayer one night that it did not matter to me if I ever got married. But if He wanted me to be, then He would have to choose her for me because, as demonstrated by my many failed relationships, my judgment was lousy. I even had the nerve to ask Him to bring her to me if that is what He wanted. In my opinion, He did and brought her to me, and unexpectedly, the very next day.

A buddy and I were at a live-music venue in Anchorage. Another friend who sometimes sang with a band there met up with us. She had invited along with her a single lady named Carmen she knew from the worship group of musicians at our church. I soon became aware of a matchmaking motive and that she had also brought Carmen to meet me with that in mind. It was unusual since, until then, a friend had never introduced me to a woman with that intent. I wasn't much attracted to this new acquaintance, nor, I supposed, was she to me. But then I remembered my prayer the night before. "OK," I thought, "I'll give this a chance." For some reason, I sensed deep down I should take a step and try to get to know her; it just felt like the right thing to do. I soon found myself very attracted to her. She was and is still beautiful in every way. I have been married to my wife, Carmen, for over twenty-three years. By that one small step, God also gave me a daughter, a son, and a son-in-law, who by His good graces are all extraordinary, and some very cool grandkids. I can love and am loved immensely. So, I gratefully acknowledge, my life has not been a complete waste.

Still, I can't help think about what I had been doing, my seemingly aimless trudge since that remarkable time God brought me some understanding and Carmen. Goodness and mercy have followed me. But was I herded onto some firmer ground to merely wander for a while? I was in my late thirties when I first started to agonize about all of this. Oddly it was not too long after I transferred back to Houston. I thought about the compromises I had made in my career choice. Should I have stuck with being a marine biologist or chosen a different vocation? I believe that God placed desires in my heart. But the problem was there were now many interests of mine. Was I to give up my career and start over to become a neuroscientist, a biblical archaeologist, or a marine geology professor? I did not know. So my default was to stay put. But I did start to focus my thoughts on what spiritual talents may be present in me. That seemed like a reasonable thing that God would want me to do.

I had heard and read that a believer should have at least one gift from the Holy Spirit. But as predicted, a conspicuous gift of mine did not come to mind. Sure, I took a few of those so-called spiritual gift tests, but they didn't show any particular one of those mentioned in the Bible standing out. They did eliminate a few things, though, assuming the test had any validity in the first place. That is my scientific mind going off. And my gut told me to be skeptical of some dogmas one could find in many of the popular self-help and often touted "Christian" books at the time. I tried to apply the prescribed confirmation methodology of having the gift affirmed by others. But I didn't know anyone, except for perhaps my biased parents, who would attest to a spiritual talent I had. Speaking of such, whether one deems them as spiritual gifts or not, I often see people who demonstrate their outstanding abilities in ways I believe glorify God, even if they are nonbelievers. "Keep up the amazing work," I say. But for me, I could not discern anything special. Other than I do think about things a lot, I'm good at being a skeptic, and I certainly love science and the outdoors.

In any case, I applied myself where I could in "church" activities and such, but few things seemed to give me as much joy as one would have expected if that was what God wanted me to do. And those few things I liked did not seem to bear much fruit as far as I could tell. I enjoyed leading a "home team," a church-related home-based social and Bible study group. My wife and I hosted one at our house. However, after a few years, the collective level of interest seemed to wane, and the attendance began to fall. So, I quit. In a way, I was glad. I wanted to be free from just another thing, of many, that seemed to oblige me to remain in the Houston area or keep me from a better life somehow or somewhere. I was no further along in discerning my calling. The dull expanse of pavement kept passing beneath my wheels. I did not know where I was going or supposed to go. But I was determined to find out.

I always had trouble falling asleep, especially during my years working in Houston, so my insomnia gave me lots of time, just about every night, to think about stuff and pray about what I should be doing with my life. Over and over, I would plead for God to let me know His will for my life, even for the slightest indication of what a single step should be, even if I didn't know where it led. But for so long, decades, I had not sensed, heard, or seen anything from God in which I thought addressed the matter. As I lay awake at night listening and waiting, I experienced only long periods of silence.

Where was that sense that God answered my prayer and was leading me in the right direction? Like when I met and married my wife so many years before. I can imagine a fellow believer saying, "Well, you just haven't been really listening or looking. God has been answering you, and you just have not heard or seen. There have probably been many doors God has opened for you." Yes! I agree, but which doors? Whether I passed or stumbled through some, I was not aware of any of them being ones that He wanted me to enter.

I did not sense I was following His specific will for my life, at least not for a very long while. One could say that is a lack of faith. And that is what I also concluded. So I prayed for more faith, continued to read the Bible, and still did not seem to have received more, at least not enough to hear any better what God may have been telling me about His plans for me. So then my thoughts also told me, "Well, then you must have sin in your life which keeps you apart from God. He will not answer your prayers for that reason." Yes, there is sin, and of which I pray for forgiveness and help to transform my life. But no matter how much I try, I keep on sinning with little sign of improvement. I was thinking about the math. If God's righteousness is perfect, then His goodness would be infinite and therefore immeasurably more than mine. My character and sin would be infinitely offensive and infinitely separate me from Him. So I have been as far away from Him as anyone could ever be. It is like my sin makes the gap as big as it can be, so the love must be grander to cover it. Or at least I see it that way. I must trust what the psalmist, King David, said, "As far as the east is from the west, so far has He removed our transgressions from us" (Psa. 103:12). What a gap Jesus covers! I certainly can't stop sinning or remove it by my sheer will, good character (yeh, right), and determination. I don't have any faith in myself at all. I <u>have</u> to trust that God did and does the work . . . and that somehow He will still lead me. My only hope is in Jesus.

CHAPTER TWO

The Road Less Traveled

I often sat "at church" on Sundays and daydreamed. I would be somewhere among snow-covered mountain peaks and snowboarding the most beautiful white powder. Or I was gliding across or drifting through a clear blue ocean, lost within the lushness of a green jungle paradise, or any place which is minimally touched by man — away from sinful contamination that is. Except there is my own. Rats! When I am in those places, I think of God . . . well, a fair bit of the time. In any case, they are my go-to spots of worship. Jesus Himself withdrew to the wilderness and a mountain to pray. If I ever got the chance, I would try to get away too.

An upside to being unemployed is that I now have more time to do so.

As of this writing, I am climbing a mountain, Denali. From here, one can get a glimpse of His greatness. Yet this massive prominence, as impressive as it is, is infinitely small in comparison to God and His power to raise it to the heavens. Still, there is something about the mountains. They are like magnificent mansions. I dream to live within them. I think we all hope to live within or experience being among the most splendid places of one kind or another. For some of us, they may be mountains or oceans. For musicians, such may be cathedrals resonating the sounds of their songs and symphonies. For others, perhaps they are warehouse-size studios with which to paint large canvases of art, astounding buildings or architecture, or auditoriums filled with eager learners. And there are even those that would see grandness in a pasture with cows. We seek such spaces and can never seem to get our fill of them quite the way we would like.

I look at photos of myself and people standing on summits. The problem is that it always takes the grandeur of the mountain and the view away. One usually sees just a small area of snow or rock. And the background is often cloudy or blurred since the person or persons were the focus. Take a picture of Denali from the Park Highway in Alaska on a clear day of the summit in June or early July. There are bound to be climbers on or near the peak, but you can't see them. As measured from its base to the top, it is widely considered the tallest land-based mountain on earth. Humans should be too small to see them on top. Now that is a proper perspective. Or take a look from the summit and see the world to a more distant horizon than you have ever seen before. That is even a better one. It is good being small enough to see something much greater. We long to experience the grandest of lives and places. The measure of their magnificence is how small we are within them.

Though I can't seem to do them enough living in Houston, I love snowboarding and surfing. And I suppose I love them both for mainly the same reason — that sense of glorious flight as I glide along a slope. On one, I fly along a rolling moonscape beneath my feet. Or as on some days, it is more like a drift through the clouds. Down I go with pulses of acceleration and deceleration as I sway in a dreamlike dance with the mountain. I can only catch a small glance and portions of her majesty as I freely explore the folds of her white dress. On the other, I ride down a local slope that develops continually and varies dynamically. I may glide across a turquoise and ever-evolving elegant curve of a face. I reach out to touch her and want to sense the force that propels me. The power of a big wave is immense. We can't fully experience it. Nor can we completely capture the grandness and majesty of mountains. Yet with these, we can get a sense of God's greatness, but it is only a glimpse.

My love for the ocean began when I was very

young. However, I grew up on the dusty High Plains of West Texas. Which is over six hundred miles from the coast. When I was seven, my parents took my sister and me to the Hemisfair, the world's fair at the time, in San Antonio. And then we went to South Padre Island at the southern tip of Texas. I recall seeing the first rows of palm trees as we drove from San Antonio toward the Texas coast. "Do you know the way to San Jose," a big hit in 1968, was playing on the radio. The song thoroughly burned its way into my memory as it played many times during the trip. When we went across the causeway and onto the barrier island, I could smell the Gulf of Mexico with its salty onshore breezes. But I could not see it for the dunes. While we headed toward our motel, my parents must have noticed me, maybe my sister too, going berserk in the back seat and decided to pull off to let us see the ocean. As soon as my dad stopped the car, I got out and ran across the dunes. And then I kept on running right into the water. The ocean was all and much more than I had expected — immense and infinite. The flat plains of West Texas seemed infinitely vast to me too, but the ocean would be so much more fun. There before me was the world's largest swimming pool. And it was heated! At least it was warm that time of year. For my height then, the waves seemed huge. And I imagined them tall as buildings the further I looked out toward the horizon. As I waded into the surf, I felt the energy of even a small wave trying to knock me down, and if I pushed my feet off the bottom at the right time, I discovered a thrilling sensation as my body would move with the swell. At the time, I could not even imagine the power of those large waves further out or how fun or terrifying it would be to experience them, especially those generated from large swells due to tropical storms entering the Gulf. The day came when I was able to paddle out there and see, and I still do.

As I sit on my surfboard in the lineup, I watch the horizon. I look for a bump or slight motion to let me know there is a chance for swell coming my way. I start to see some lines in the far distance to my left, but the swell direction is also to my left, so those waves will not be for me. Hope builds anyway because a line of swell in the area indicates a set is coming. I see then some waves are coming my way. Am I in the right spot? Or am I too shallow? It is frustrating to see a beautiful wave break just beyond where you should be to catch it. And then I pay for my mistake as it pounds me on the head as it rolls by. During large offshore storms, a set of swells can appear suddenly. And I realize I am too shallow for the big waves that are coming. The first swell will pass me by underneath as it lifts me several feet and then lowers me gently. The next line usually rises ahead as a wall of water with a steeper face. I paddle anxiously to get into position, only to realize I am too late. So I duck dive under as it breaks. But what is terrifying is just before going under, I often hear what sounds like a freight train I can't see just beyond the mountain of water I am trying to avoid. When I emerge, I quickly inhale some air and brace myself, knowing I am about to be hit by a torrent of whitewash from a second wave. The impact then tumbles me over and over underwater. By the time I can finally come up and catch my breath, the best waves have already passed by me. I hear the joyous hollers of others that caught the wave of their lives. I wait and hope again for another set, another chance . . . for it to be my turn.

To consider the expanse of the ocean and look out to its horizon is fascinating. It is like where our minds go while gazing intently at the heavens' faintest shimmers on a clear dark night. We wonder about the infinite. But on the ocean, we can reach its furthest shores and beyond what we can see or know. And to move seemingly without limits across a pristine azure surface while being gently washed by its warm salty spray, is to me, the allure of sailing. There is also that child-like feeling of being caught out in the rain without caring. We splash about in one big puddle. A few opportunities to sail have allowed me to escape the constraints and sight of private property and pavement. So for me to get to go where I please and not experience boundaries or obstructions is heaven. Fortunately, there are livable land-based regions that can give one that impression.

Norway comes to mind. I was also able to live there as part of my career. But it was only briefly for about one year. In Norway, you can be driving along and see a mountain peak, and if you want, you can go there and climb or snowboard it. Just close any gates you encounter behind you. No one will stop you. If you would like to go to a beach, you may hike across the field, dunes, whatever, and play in the sand. I even went surfing there. All the things I loved to do were in Norway — even diving.

Two-dimensional freedom is bliss, but an even greater joy is to be able to move in three dimensions with ease. Diving within the ocean is like floating . . . falling . . . but more like flying through the immense blue — weightless. I can move effortlessly through beautiful kelp gardens and along rock formations that generate the most pleasurable experience, similar to the one I get within my most recurrent dreams in which I can easily float up or down. When looking and moving down, sun rays penetrate and highlight a tunnel-like path below me. The bottom comes suddenly into view, and I experience the marvelous color of the reef and its variety of marine life. The mystery the ocean provides has always fascinated me. It is vastly unknown and easily provokes the imagination about what lies just beyond what you can see. As a deepwater exploration geologist, I have peered through the ocean depths and sediments on a computer screen and chosen the position to sink wells through the seafloor and deep into the earth's crust. All of which enlightens one with knowledge of the ocean and what lies beneath its great depths. But it is nothing like being immersed in its grand theater.

There is indeed an allure of the deep and the unknown that draws me. Once while diving, I followed the sunlit corridor down until I sensed the tunnel beginning to darken and close in on me. Suddenly, I felt very uneasy and a bit lightheaded with almost a vertigo-type sensation. I imagined if I went any further, I would be spun like in a whirlpool and dragged down into the abyss. I was 154 feet down and within a steep-walled canyon just offshore the tip of the Baja California Peninsula. Far below me was my dive guide motioning me to come deeper. Earlier in the boat, he mentioned that he had been a champion freediver. He was more used to these depths than I was. I chose to live instead and made my way up slowly toward the light. The blue, with all its apparent freedom in three dimensions, was very enticing. But there are boundaries to what one should do with such liberty. Freedom is beautiful. I learned it could also drag you down, crush you, and just as soon kill you. Other than God's grace, I'm not sure how I have made it this far. My freedom to make choices as an adult has allowed me to make awful ones that have dragged me down, crushed my soul, and could easily justify my death, even by my measure. At times I feel I have dived too far and am still there in the abyss. How does one escape such a place where one surrounds oneself with complete absence? There is no light and not the slightest sense of God.

But there in the darkness and the silence, I realized the dark silence was the message — the answer itself and not the absence of one. My thinking was wrong the whole time. Faith is not about knowing beforehand. Why would receiving a sense of direction be any different? Even if faith is blind and deaf in a way, I'm not lost. I do not know the direction I'm going until I take one. Faith is what it takes for me to move. From the depths, you must move perchance to reach the shallows. Though, to get there, I may tend to sink down and then try to crawl upslope along the bottom. From the shallows, you can then reach the shore. And on the land, you can walk. I do not know what the next step is until I take that step, any step. I may not know where I am going, but God does. I must trust that He will lead me to good pastures even without me knowing anything else. I had questioned myself earlier about having some sense of God leading me in the right direction, like when I met my wife. I forgot something critical. I had trusted first and not the other way around. I did not meet Carmen, and only then trust Him. Instead, I had let go and trusted God first without any sense at all about whether He would lead me to marriage. Had I received an answer from the start about where I was supposed to go, directions to my destination, then I would not need faith, and arguably I would not need to be led there. It is as if God wants to be present and take me there Himself. I must trust and walk to go with Him. He is the shepherd. Good pastures will come.

Therefore, I have found I should not worry about me achieving awareness of my destiny or unique purpose, that one thing. I have a purpose, but carrying it out does not require having some direction beforehand or knowing at each moment what that purpose is. I accept, in general, our lives are about glorifying Him. And I am reminded of the overarching command to love as found in His Word. Loving someone is always a good idea when you are not feeling useful. Maybe the prophet Micah hit it on the head, "He has told you, O [Old] man, what is good [Hah!]; and what does the Lord require of you but to do justice, to love kindness, and to walk humbly with your God?" (Micah 6:8, my words in brackets).

In any case, I exist for God's purpose. He will work through me or not through me as He wills. He deals with us as He chooses. Somehow by His grace, He chooses, and then I may choose. I am free, yet He accomplishes His will. He is sovereign, yes the cliché is true, and I am free. A paradox, I know. It is hard to explain, but I think resolving it has something to do with God's love. As a mere human,

I can't fully understand the matter. I only know in my relationship with my wife, I desire for her to love me, but I want her to be free to love me. I can pursue her and court her and work hard in building a relationship with her, but I would not want her to love me because she does not have other opportunities. And I don't want her to love me because it is her duty either. Perhaps one of the greatest glories of love is being given the freedom to love. Doesn't God have the will and power to do that for us, even being sovereign? Furthermore, what if all options and experiences, even horrible ones, were available to us, some seemingly pressed on us — would we, could we, love and be in love with God? Maybe He wants us to be able to love Him on not just His terms but as much on our terms and will as possible.

I believe I am free, yet He may accomplish His will and His unique purpose for me and through me, as he chooses, whether I am aware of it or not. As Jesus said, "The wind blows where it wishes and you hear the sound of it, but do not know where it comes from and where it is going; so is everyone who is born of the Spirit" (John 3:8). I am also not saying that a willing heart is not beneficial. God's grace in dealing with us to get us to that point glorifies Him. "Abide in Me, and I in you. As the branch cannot bear fruit of itself unless it abides in the vine, so neither can you unless you abide in Me" (John 15:4). Likewise, "Draw near to God and He will draw near to you" (James 4:8). Changed lives testify to that. And not only those transformations, but a specific sense of purpose is certainly evident to many. I have heard people affirm knowing their calling and have witnessed it being carried out superbly in their ministries and careers. So some know, others do not. Therefore, I do not believe we can put God in a box about whether or how He reveals His work or his plans to us. God does not abide by our formulas.

I am a bit ashamed for spending so much time being concerned about God's specific will for my life. It seems like such an entitled attitude from a person to whom so much privilege has been given, while others have only known suffering, disease, hunger, and thirst. And when there are millions of children and young men and women who die early and unexpectedly in life. What about those living on the streets, abandoned by their family, and trying to survive? Or what about the people I have personally known whose plans were tragically suddenly ended, some even violently? I should be grateful to be doing anything. The apostle Paul alludes to that idea in saying, "Whatever you do in word or deed, do all in the name of the Lord Jesus, giving thanks through Him to God the Father" (Col. 3:17). Even getting to wonder and to wander is to be appreciated.

In one way or another, perhaps I have been led like the Israelites in a barren land, not knowing my direction all those years, to humble me. To them, Moses taught, "You shall remember all the way which the Lord your God has led you in the wilderness these forty years, that He might humble you, testing you, to know what was in your heart, whether you would keep His commandments or not" (Deut. 8:2). That last part hurts. I didn't keep His commandments. And I don't think it was for Him to know my heart, but for me to know my heart. That is humbling.

Once as a child, I sat down between the rails of an old ladder that lay in the yard and scooped up the fallen dead leaves all around me as far as I could reach them and buried myself. From within this heap, I readied myself with my knees bent and my feet firmly planted against the rungs, which were now the peddles of my newly constructed space module. I squinted a little, and the world began to blur around me into a beautiful array of colors. I believed I had created a machine that would magically transport me to some marvelous place. And looking back, I guess it did in a way. But after fully opening my eyes, I saw I had gone nowhere. I thought my imagination and effort would somehow create a reality and take me there, somewhere else. I remember being so disappointed in the failure to achieve the result for which I was hoping, which was supposed to happen. Such are dreams. Even so, hopes and dreams motivate us, keep us moving when all seems lost. While on a hike recently in the mountains, the fluttering leaves of the aspens caught my attention. And then I felt the wind blow right by me just like it was time. Time, for sure, time for me to not consider further its passing, but to move onward.

CHAPTER THREE

"Monster Wrastle"

When my children were young, we would play a game I called "monster wrastle." I meant monster wrestle, but I never said it that way. I would get in bed and under the sheet and pretend to be a monster. My kids would pounce on me from above, and I would grab, wrestle, and tickle them as they then tried to get away from me. What I liked most about the game was getting to hug and love them while they imagined something much different. In some sense, perhaps God loves us that way too. We can't fathom the reach or magnitude of His love or imagine the true nature of the "beast" *(meant fondly)*, but I think He enjoys our trust and "wrastling" with Him, that being who does seem somewhat cloaked for now.

Thinking back, I wished those days would have lasted forever because as my children got older, the hugs were fewer and fewer. I have always heard you have control of your kids until they are eighteen. Or maybe one says it's thirty now. In any case, it's not true. I think most of us parents only have them for about twelve years, and then they somehow manage to slip our grip . . . or at least for a while. Of course, I'm trying to be funny here more than emphatic. But some separation happens. The brains of teenagers prune, rewire, and reconstruct themselves, while I think the reptilian part remains intact or seems to dominate. Occasionally then, my kids reacted to me in such a way I must have come across to them as a monster. Or at least in a manner having little to remind them of a benevolent father still there beneath the frightful look. Even with all the disconnections going on, most of us at that age begin to seriously try to process who or what we want to be when we grow up. And at some point, we tend to question everything, including what we believe. And we should. Even Paul said, "Examine everything *carefully*; hold fast to that which is good" (1 Thess. 5:21). If we merely accept what others tell us, and never question it, then we may never really know. And it is good to be allowed to know. Left alone to find some answers also tests our hearts, as I found out. Examining all includes me questioning my thinking as well, but I need the space to do so. As caring parents, we understand that the separation helps prepare our children to become who they choose to be as adults. We raise them to be ably away in one sense, yet we want them to stay close in another. But they remain as our child regardless and grow up in our love, whether they realize it or not. And we hope that love and the best of our character embed themselves deeply, and the training we provided guide them in every proper way. They may not fathom the extent of our love, but we hope they ultimately understand they can't escape its grasp.

At times, though, I still have doubts and feel vastly separated from my Father. Especially when I sin and callously ignore I am His. Then I think I will miss out on all the good things he has to offer me. Perhaps those blessings are now too far out of reach. My efforts to recover them by obedience will be vain. They will be tainted and dismissed due to being mainly done out of a sense of obligation and fear. Have I also negated what could have been mine in the Father's house in heaven? But I have realized my misunderstandings are often born out of listening to the wrong voices . . . and listening to me. I had accepted that the way for me to heaven is through Christ. But I also had been thoroughly impressed with the notion that I had better behave in the meantime. Or else I would not experience the Lord's goodness. Or worse, by some lapse on my part, the door, I thought will be opened, would remain shut!

Since then, I have come to believe I know the

Lord better than that, yet I remain ignorant about much, and often willfully so. Has my understanding still been darkened, my heart hardened? Paul warned us not to be like those "excluded from the life of God because of the ignorance that is in them" (Eph. 4:18). I have hidden my face, but when I come to Him baring myself fully, why does it often seem He hides His face even then? Do the words of the prophet Isaiah still apply after all? "Your sins have hidden *His* face from you so that He does not hear" (Isa. 59:2). And even to Moses, the Lord said, "I will put you in the cleft of the rock and cover you with My hand until I have passed by. Then I will take My hand away and you shall see My back, but My face shall not be seen" (Exo. 33:22–23). So I questioned further and found Isaiah wrote, "[Shall] what is formed say to him who formed it, 'He has no understanding?'" (Isa. 29:16). And then Isaiah added these prophetic words, "In that day shall the deaf hear the words of the book, and the eyes of the blind shall see out of obscurity, and out of darkness" (Isa. 29:18, KJV). But what words was he referring to? I may be in the dark for a moment, and there are things I will not see for now. I only get a glimpse. But whether I hide my face or He hides His, or I journey far away from my Father, I am His child and should still be heir to everything good He has for me. Right? Or could I have lost that privilege, and I do not know it?

And then I think of my children. I want them to have joy and the very best for them, whether they are near to me or not. And I am closer than they think anyway. So our closeness and love for each other are not really about hugs and feelings or their behaviors toward me. When my children, out of their freedom, show nobility, courage, and selflessness in loving and caring for others, and they have mightily, they love and honor me, perhaps more than they will ever know in this life. But whatever they do, they are still my children anyway. And they are His as I am. They have the very best of what I have to offer them — the same love from the Father that I received. And when they express that love to others, I can't think of a better way to love me back. They have not lost any privileges with me. So I trust it is that way with my Father. He is always extending His arms and sometimes taking hold of me, yet I often did not fully understand who or with what I was wrestling.

So we wait eagerly for longer days, a coming home, and a better understanding. A place we get our questions answered. We are united and mature, but the youth of our childhood, our innocence, and joy can last forever. I want a home where we have our lives fulfilled. I can love and spend time with my family and not tire. And there are laughter and "monster wrastling" until the day is done. I think I will also need a dwelling large enough to move around and freely be who I am supposed to be. Somewhere I will truly live and be content to remain forever with God. Only He can provide such a place. Like King David who prayed, "One thing I have asked from the Lord, that I shall seek: that I may dwell in the house of the Lord all the days of my life" (Psa. 27:4).

CHAPTER FOUR

"The Father's Mansion"

I have read many times Jesus' words, "In my Father's house are many mansions; if *it* were not *so*, I would have told you; I go to prepare a place for you" (John 14:2, KJV). I have taken hold of that hope and have tried to envision the details. I wish I could see for myself from a high mountain, like John, the writer of the book of Revelation, the holy city, the tabernacle of God among us, coming down from heaven with the brilliant glory of God. That place where He will wipe away every tear, where there is no longer any death, crying, or pain, along with having the enormity of being fifteen hundred miles in length, width, and height as the writer describes (Rev. 21:4, 10–11, 16). Such a size would have a volume of over three billion cubic miles — a space that could easily have over four hundred billion rooms, and each is as large as our biggest football stadiums with vast areas to spare. That is a lot of construction. Not the type of work I would want to do. Thankfully, Jesus said He was going to prepare a place.

In the longness of the night, I at least had some consolation of someday inhabiting the tremendous home that He was preparing for me in heaven if nothing else. As if it was some ultimate hedge to make up for my failed earthly life, a far better place than the one I had. As Paul said, "For indeed in this *house* we groan longing to be clothed with our dwelling from heaven" (2 Cor. 5:2). Still, it seemed to be such a dim view. An uneasiness remained as I turned from side to side in my bed. But then a faint light, just a glint, came through in the darkness. And it was enough to change my thinking. Some of Jesus' words had come to mind. And then I realized, or at least I began to believe, the place He was speaking of preparing was not necessarily in heaven, at least not the way I had thought. I should have been considering a dwelling, not in heaven, but from heaven and much closer to my present home.

Jesus spoke of going to prepare a place in His Father's house. But just a few verses later, He said, "In that day you will know that I am in My Father, and you in Me, and I in you" (John 14:20). So Jesus goes to prepare a place at His Father's house. Where is that? He is in the Father, and Christ is in me. The place that Jesus went to prepare is in me. That magnificent mansion is within me! And with Christ in me preparing the Father's house, then this presents a glorious expectation. That is a new, even better, hope than I had envisioned previously. Paul seemed to make the point most intriguingly:

> *That is,* the mystery which has been hidden from the past ages and

> generations, but has now been manifested to His saints, to whom God willed to make known what is the riches of the glory of this mystery among the Gentiles, which is Christ in you, the hope of glory. (Col. 1:26–27)

But his words did not quite register until now. Since my childhood, I have heard Jesus comes into our hearts and lives when we accept Him as our Lord and Savior. I understood that sort of, but somehow a disconnect was there in my thinking. I took it more as a figure of speech than reality. Since accepting friends, relatives, or pets into my life meant mainly having to spend time with or caring for them, why would the Lord be any different? And the stuff about the heart, I treated the notion no better than a feeling I should have or a welcoming attitude. Or maybe, it was akin to the clichés, to keep one "in my heart" or "in my thoughts and prayers." And I understood, or at least heard, that

He affects or works in us in some way. Or, as believers, we are supposed to obey His commandments in the Bible and represent Him as best as we can. But His actual presence in me, being His house, is another matter. I realize now this is not merely a metaphor. Nor is His dwelling a meager residence, such as a small apartment I share with Him in which he quietly resides. One in which I may bug Him for something like an annoying roommate — all while I wait for a better place in heaven. Instead, I believe He is there in me to build a more stately residence now. Even as big as He is, we both somehow fit along with the Father in His house. But wait, there's more! Jesus said,

> I will ask the Father, and He will give you another Helper, that He may be with you forever *that is* the Spirit of truth, whom the world cannot receive, because it does not see Him or know Him, *but* you know Him because He abides with you and will

be in you. (John 14:16–17)

And in case I missed that, Paul reaffirms this more precisely with the delivery of a double punch. "Do you not know that you are a temple of God and *that* the Spirit of God dwells in you?" (1 Cor. 3:16). And with regards to Christ, "For in Him all the fullness of Deity dwells in bodily form" (Col. 2:9). These words seem to suggest more than mere notions of intimacy. With Christ in us, we are the actual temple of God.

What I had read in the book of Isaiah was true: "In that day shall the deaf hear the words of the book." I had recalled from the Gospel of John what Jesus said, "In that day you will know that I am in My Father, and you in Me, and I in you." That day I heard the words of a book. And like Isaiah predicted, "the eyes of the blind will see out of obscurity, and out of darkness," I too finally saw. The prayer of David, that "one thing I have asked," is also answered. We will, indeed, "dwell in the house of the Lord all the days of [our] life." There is no need to wait for heaven. God abides in us today and is always with us. What a mansion! But the measure of its magnificence is how small I am within it. The lesser my natural self can be, the grander the dwelling. The greatest I can think of is God's love, and His love within me is the measure of my significance.

Christ said He goes to prepare a place. And in His very next words, He also says, "If I go and prepare a place for you, I will come again and receive you to Myself, that where I am, *there* you may be also" (John 14:3). I read it would have been customary in Jewish marriages at that time for the groom to go and prepare a room for the bride and him to live at his father's house. But the groom would not return to fetch his bride until his father determined the room was ready. Does this mean there could be some delay? My place does seem such a mess. But then I think of Jesus going to the cross. He has prepared a place for me, and He, the resurrected Christ, has returned. Because of what He did, I believe I can be where He is and rest on the good news that Christ has done what was necessary to move in. And it is He who cleaned it up. Jesus also added, "If anyone loves Me, he will keep My word; and My Father will love him, and We will come to him and make Our abode with him" (John 14:23). He does not say that He and the Father will make their abode apart from us, and then they will come. Instead, they will make their abode with us, anyone that loves Him. So we have this hope now. But there is continuing work, not to declare us clean, but to build a home in us that will reveal the "riches of His glory." We have His helper, the Spirit, as well. His house includes many mansions. So this is no standard home. It is one He has prepared and continues to make with us. And He will reveal it throughout His whole kingdom in a way I can't fully imagine. In this place, we can see Him the way He intends for us to see Him.

Little children, by the way, must have an idea of

such a place already. Besides tending to have things more in order, I think, being small, they have a more proper perspective. My guess is they see the world as it is supposed to be and not as it is in its current earthly state. They seem to generate their awe and joy about life and everything from an essence totally within themselves and worry about nothing. We, adults, see the present world as it appears to us from our experience and not as it is supposed to be. Maybe that is why Jesus said, "For the kingdom of God belongs to such as these. Truly I say to you, whoever does not receive the kingdom of God like a child will not enter it at all" (Luke 18:16–17). If only I could become young again. Perhaps, that is what happens.

CHAPTER FIVE

Preparing a Place

On the most crevasse riddled portions of Denali, we traveled across them only during the coldest hours after sundown with the hope the snow bridges were frozen firm enough to pass safely over. During one of these nights, I was made eerily aware of how the relative dimness changed my perspective from the daytime. The mountains were marked with jagged streaks of snow against their gray bluish-black rocks, as though their sides bled by being slashed with daggers. When viewed through some clouds, their slopes vaguely transformed into the heavens. And only in the light that came near dawn, the white-gray sky was demarcated by contrast to the pure-white snow. The loneliness and utter deadliness the mountains were portraying struck me. There was a darker side to the valley.

On our descent, we had to cross back over a long glacier of this valley. But what had been a smooth route with a well-marked and firmly packed trail was now a sea of crevasses. Within a period of just a few days, the warmer sunny days we had enjoyed as we headed to the summit transformed its surface. As we descended to this broad crevasse field, it was getting close to dawn, and our lead guide deemed the ice bridges too soft to continue. We were supposed to get back to the airstrip and fly back to the airbase in Talkeetna that day. I was looking very forward to meeting up with my wife there, whom I had not seen in about a month. The thought of the delay in seeing her gave me a sick feeling. We decided to make camp with other teams who had stopped previously in a broad patch of unbroken terrain on the glacier. The guides used a long pole to probe out a safe area for setting up the tents with the expectation we could be there a good while. We made camp and tried to sleep for the remainder of the day. Around midnight we heard from our lead guide that the temperatures had fallen slightly and the snow was firming up. He decided we should take our chances. Our climb down began again at 2:00 am. The descent over the rough surface of the glacier was a slow zigzag journey behind our guide. Carefully he would lie on his belly and probe with a long rod for firm ice bridges and hidden crevasses. I prayed we would all make it through safely. After a night of stumbling, some falls arrested by being roped to other team members, and sleds nose-diving into crevasses followed by much cursing, we managed to make it safely past the most dangerous portions of the crevasse field by dawn. All along, I had put complete trust in my guide. He was the one scouting out the most deadly dangers along a route, and we survived. The sun broke from behind a mountain with such a beautiful light.

Making it past the gnarliest part restored my hope in getting to the airstrip that morning and flying out. I would finally get to see my wife. At times like these, I think of how much she means to me. Besides God's grace, having her in my life is the best thing that has ever happened to me, yet even that is part of His doing. Within this short life and my imperfect character, my prayer is that I will be good for her. And that somehow she receives all the love I should have for her. But I know my natural self has never done any good. If any good does come from me, then it would have to be something God was doing. So my best plan is to let Him come through. For her to receive the best of all the love she should have from me, I must offer His.

Things worked out. I made it to where I was supposed to be with my wife. And we all safely made it back home from the mountain because we trusted our guide, albeit with some fear and trembling. Similarly, I trust in Jesus. He not only knows the way; He is the way. I do not need to do anything to be welcome within His house or have access to His glory, but to realize I may enter His temple because of the work He has done. "The veil of the temple was torn in two from top to bottom" (Matt. 27:51), and most definitely not by me, not bottom to top, not by my hand in any way.

But I also believe God does not leave me there, just standing within the entrance. He is the greatest of hosts. I will not only get to banquet with Him, but I will also live with and know Him. Maybe God wants me to understand more about what He has prepared for me. However, I think I will need to get out of my usual head for a change.

My earthly father taught me that it doesn't matter much what happens to you in this life, but how you think about it. There is a blunt truth to that. But how do I think about things the right way? "I know, O Lord, that a man's way is not in himself, nor is it in a man who walks to direct his steps" (Jer. 10:23). I must put my natural thinking aside, but how can that be? Paul admonished the church in

Rome to "not be conformed to this world, but be transformed by the renewing of your mind, so that you may prove what the will of God is, that which is good and acceptable and perfect" (Rom. 12:2). And to the Philippians, he said, "Whatever is true, whatever is honorable, whatever is right, whatever is pure, whatever is lovely, whatever is of good repute, if there is any excellence and if anything worthy of praise, dwell on these things" (Phil. 4:8). But again, what must I do for this to occur and renew my mind to cause the transformation? Paul also stood before a bunch of skeptics like myself in Athens and said,

> The God who made the world and all things in it, since He is Lord of heaven and earth, does not dwell in temples made with hands; nor is He served by human hands, as though He needed anything, since He Himself gives to all

people life and breath and all things. (Acts 17:24–25)

Paul reaches a climax in his discourse as he beautifully states, "For in Him we live, and move, and have our being" (Acts 17:28, KJV). So much is in his speech. What part of "nor is He served by human hands," "He Himself gives to all people life and breath and all things," and "in Him we live and move and have our being" do I not understand? I don't need to do anything. Can't He provide the transformation by the renewing of my mind? I think what Paul was saying is let it so be. God doesn't need me or you to do anything, yet that would seem to go against our natural grain, our usual way of thinking. The writer of the book of Hebrews urges us to "also lay aside every encumbrance and the sin which so easily entangles us, and let us run with endurance the race that is set before us" (Heb. 12:1). Yes, we should run the race that way and dwell on things most noble. But I don't believe we do any of those things apart from God and His work in us. Paul points out our worldly thoughts and inclinations contrast with the things of God that we also can't know, except by His Spirit:

> "Things which eye has not seen and ear has not heard, and *which* have not entered the heart of man, all that God has prepared for those who love Him." For to us God revealed *them* through the Spirit; for the Spirit searches all things, even the depths of God. For who among men knows the *thoughts* of a man except the spirit of the man which is in him? Even so the *thoughts* of God no one knows except the Spirit of God. Now we have received, not the spirit of the world, but the Spirit who is from God, so that we may know the things freely given to us by God, which things we also speak, not in words taught by human wisdom, but in those taught by the Spirit, combining spiritual *thoughts* with spiritual *words*. But a natural

> man does not accept the things of the Spirit of God, for they are foolishness to him; and he cannot understand them, because they are spiritually appraised. (1 Cor. 2:9–14)

The words indicate the Holy Spirit teaches us, brings about our new minds, to know the things of God, which He reveals to us about Himself. Thus, minds that discern anything of Him and accord to His ways do not come from our effort. Nor can we perceive and accept things of Him by our natural wisdom or human logic, but only by the Spirit. "For it is God who is at work in you, both to will and to work for *His* good pleasure" (Phil. 2:13). Therefore, just as we can rest on His grace, we can lean and rely on Him who is in us.

Back in the time of the prophet Haggai, the temple lay desolate. And a message came by the prophet to the Jews saying, "'Thus says the Lord of hosts, Consider your ways! Go up to the mountains, bring wood and rebuild the temple, that I may be pleased with it and be glorified'" (Hag. 1:7–8). The Lord would seem to take pleasure in not just His house but the rebuilding of it by His people. Yet Christ does the work in us for that temple. But does He enjoy our willing hearts and our companionship in the process? I once built a backyard playset for my son. I knew he was too young to help me with the task. But what a joy to see him hang out with me, watch what I was building, and his willingness to be of use, though I may have overly expressed my frustration in trying to show him how. As a mere mortal being, I could have been more sensitive. But yes, I think so. As a child, I would spend hours in my dad's shop and watch him create a sculpture from wood or rock. I was always amazed to see the transformation into what he was making. Our Father does not need us to do anything, but wouldn't He want us to be around Him close enough to reveal what He has prepared and is making for us?

I have often noticed mountain peaks that come into view only partially above or between the clouds. In such cases, my perception or imagination tends to make them much larger or taller than their earthly reality. They are still tremendous, no doubt. But at least they can be climbed, and we can get some sense of their physical measure. But in terms of spiritual realities, I think the opposite is true. My guess is our perceptions and imaginations of them and efforts to reach up and grasp them tend to fall way short. And, for me, that lack drives my thirst to know. We want to see what God was and is doing, and perhaps we will soon enough. But I suspect things will be quite different from what we think.

CHAPTER SIX

The Revealing

My grandfather, "Shorty," dreamed of having cows, a bit of pasture, and a dairy operation again after a careless individual dumped buckets of lead paint next to his fence that led to the death of all his cows. As a result, he lost the farm and then spent many years driving a milk truck while all along carrying the hope to earn just enough money for a day that he could make a down payment on a small plot of land. Finally, he reached that day. He left early that morning to deliver the last loads of milk. As he drove down the highway, he topped a hill. It was a place he knew well and thought about much because its crest revealed the location where his three-year-old daughter Valli had died years earlier in the car due to complications from whooping cough. But on this day, he noticed a truck there which had broken down in the middle of the highway. A man and a teenager were waving to flag him down. Shorty pulled up beside them and invited them to join him in his truck and offered to drive them into town for help. They got into the cab next to him. Then they attacked and dragged him out of his seat and into some tall weeds near the road. There they stabbed him over and over, even as he offered them all of his money and pleaded not to kill him. Shorty crawled around and around with blood gushing from over fifteen knife wounds in his body for over half an hour before he died. "This is all God's will," a strange lady said callously to his wife, Betty, my grandmother. The woman had come uninvited into the house where she and my mom were right before Shorty's funeral. With a Bible in her hand, she began to talk down to my grandmother. "This is God's will for your life!" she insisted. "He's sent me here to clarify the mystery." My mom, who was just twenty-two at the time, responded to the irritating woman, "Better to suffer a mystery. Better to leave everything well enough alone than besmirch the character of God . . . . Besides, you don't know anything. Two little boys have just lost their daddy. A teenager's life is messed up." In the middle of dealing with her own father's death, a dad she loved dearly, it was <u>the murderers and their families</u> for whom my mom had concern and compassion. My mom had learned personal details of the young men, both black, one a twenty-six-year-old and a father of two boys, and a sixteen-year-old through police reports and newspaper clippings. The news had been out quickly since officers caught them within hours of the murder after someone saw the two leave the stolen milk truck. At the police station, they both broke down and confessed everything. They readily gave the gory details of the killing and even spoke of Shorty's pleading. The night before his funeral, at midnight, my mother felt she needed to go to the funeral home to be alone with her dad. While she was there in the dismal cold room beside his casket, she reached out and touched his hand. She drew it back in horror because of how rigid and cold it felt. In the depths of her misery, she collapsed to her knees and leaned her head against the coffin. But she could not pray. Within a few moments, she sensed some light and a feeling of warmth she could not explain penetrate the stark chill. Somehow, she was suddenly at peace and knew everything would be OK. She smiled and thought of how happy her dad must be to see Valli and about his dream. She hoped that cows were there.

As I read my mom's memoirs and recalled many conversations with her, I was amazed. I saw God's love shining through in my mother when it was least expected. She never expressed an ounce of hate toward those who killed her dad. Through all the years, I have only heard of her compassion for the murderers and their families. I never got the sense my mom was ever hung-up worrying about her unique purpose or about how God was specifically going to use her. When she wrote of the events surrounding her father's death, she would not have known that a mere conversation she had with an annoying proselytizing lady would move someone such as me so much. Christ's definitive work showed up in my mom and a most unusual moment. In her words, I believe I heard His voice.

And God's glory, his building, shone through in the life of Shorty. He faithfully loved and cared for a schizophrenic wife who was often abusive and dismissive of him, all while raising three children practically by himself. I wish I had known my grandfather. My mom knew him as a humble man who was always cheerful, full of goodness, and kind to strangers. He was without a prejudiced bone in his body — even though prejudice toward blacks was prevalent and segregation was considered normal among his fellow white rural Texans in the 1950s. Shorty had no problem being with or seen with people of any color in his cab or anywhere. A pasture with some cows would have been a grand place for a humble man, but I have to believe there truly is an even more stately one for Shorty and us all that Christ builds in us. I am in awe as I am reminded of Christ's craftsmanship in people by way of the simplest expressions of compassion, the sacrifice of love, the presence of peace, the throwing away of all prejudice — no matter what the cost.

My grandmother Betty was institutionalized twice and received over a hundred electric shock treatments for her schizophrenia. While in the hospital, she would often send letters to her family. She once wrote:

> I am no good at talking, but I sure do want my kiddies to have a place in the Son shine. I know He is that light. I'm gladly bending my knee to Him. The Lord is not satisfied to leave me in the dim

> twilight in which I first met Him but is at pains to lead me into a fuller light. Christ continually looms up ever greater and more wonderful.

It is interesting to note that in the uttermost darkness of her insanity and with likely cognitive impairment from the shocks to the frontal lobe portions of her brain, her words about God were the most coherent. She spoke of the Lord being "at pains" to lead her out of the dim twilight in which she first met Him into a "fuller" light. I can't imagine the sorrow, confusion, and isolation she endured or her experiences through the hellish therapies she underwent. But I suspect her pain and His pain were one. In choosing the word "twilight," was she thinking of a moment in the faint light before dawn or in the very late evening of her life? Only she and the Lord could know how she reckoned the time or the thought put into her words. Yet within her flawed mind, it was clear she expected to see a more glorious light, even if it was late in her day. But moments of Christ's work and His glory within us are infinitely significant, no matter how few and how little time our mortal flesh has left, in comparison to the utter meaninglessness of having no such moments. The presence of such in our dying bodies is the joyful pain of life. Paul wrote, "We have this treasure in earthen vessels, so that the surpassing greatness of the power will be of God and not from ourselves. . . . Therefore we do not lose heart, but though our outer man is decaying, yet our inner man is being renewed day by day" (2 Cor. 4:7,16).

Sometimes it is late in the day and our life, and the twilight is all one may have. But at least there is still light. I had the privilege to spend a significant portion of three days with my brother-in-law Ray before he died from esophageal cancer that had spread throughout his body. I got to know and connect with him more in those three days than I had in twenty-three years of knowing him in the busyness of life. Ray was a very approachable and likable guy. He was young at heart, intelligent, compassionate, and funny. He always made me laugh. To meet him was to make one smile. But amid his weakness and pain, someone more than I had known was there and to whom I was drawn. His throat was mostly obstructed and aflame from the effects of the cancer and its harsh treatments. The idea of the taste and cool soothing relief of a cherry Icee, a drink he loved, came to his mind. He was delighted to hear I would go to get him one. I drove urgently to a convenience store, but it did not have them. I went to two others and still had no luck. My heart ached at the delay and the idea of not delivering that small comfort. I ended up getting him a red slushy of some sort. He graciously thanked me and smiled as he took a couple of sips, and then he set it aside. My heart broke in failing to serve him the drink he had so desired. He passed away shortly afterward. But for some reason, I was most aware of my grief and sense of losing Ray in my frantic drive to find an Icee. Was it because I was away from the person I got to know at that time and missing him, or what? There is something about such a condition that can reveal the holiness of a person. Illnesses tend to get us out of our preoccupation with the material and our everyday experiences. In the most severe cases, they seem to strip off the flesh or at least all the faith we have in the benefits of our carnal life. In many ways, they bring us back to a glorious state. I think that is why babies are so attractive. Their innocence draws us to them. So it is in times of death. On that day, Ray told me he was the luckiest man alive. I believe, in him, I saw the glory of Christ. I also witnessed how the life of my sister, Ray's wife, was rebuilt from such devastation. Some elements of her faith were stripped, such as the stale and useless bits. Or they became reshaped. Critical ones, the anchor rods, were added or strengthened further as if God was reinforcing the foundation He laid within her through it all.

The testaments of the victims and the survivors, and the heroic presence in them, have moved me. For many attest to rising to a new faith. I have heard one report his awakening to a more joyous morning than he has ever known. But I have also known friends and believers whose lives ended abruptly and very tragically and did not seem to have received any comfort or even had the chance. Yet there are the witnesses and those within earshot of their dolor, such as I have been. And in the lack of resolution, I sense a stronger or greater kind of faith is still available for us, for the whole body of Christ. Perhaps the reliance on the sheer bareness of hope brings us to that view. Much of my faith in God has been built, not from knowing, but from not knowing. So maybe a grander perspective to be revealed awaits for us more than we can imagine.

I am grateful to have seen Christ's work in so many people in my life. His demonstration of love, patience, and grace through my wife Carmen was always there before me. Plus, I receive the benefits of her contentment and awe-inspiring talent as a musician. I have seen His preparation within my family and many of those I love, even though sometimes the circumstances surrounding that revealing were horrific. God can and will build His mansions and His holy body, the Church, from the rubble of seemingly unfulfilled, wasted, and even devastated lives. But when will we know fully about all the things that God has prepared for us who love Him? In light of what Paul wrote, "For to us God revealed *them* through the Spirit," one could assume His children would each and already know all that God has prepared for him or her. Or was Paul talking about us in a more collective sense, His body, the Church?

I believe God builds his grand home, the Church, through the lives of its members. Each room, He carefully constructs. Some are made seemingly fast, others slowly. Some are in full view. And in some, the work is revealed only subtly. Some are built through longsuffering or in great mourning. Some arise from utter destruction, while others are from the strongest of foundations. Some are in the mid of night, and some in a morning's joy. Some involve the demolishment of the evilest of hearts, and some, perhaps, are made even through a long silence. All is revealed, all that He has prepared for us, to glorify the one most deserving, His beloved Son.

Jesus said, "He who has seen Me has seen the Father" (John 14:9). God does not hide His face. With Christ expressed through us, we are His face. It is Him one sees when He loves through us because we are His body. But He is not just where I am at, around here, my group, my side, or my side of the border. His children, our brothers, and our neighbors are everywhere. He is where He chooses to be. His kingdom is not of this world, so when I see Him, He is not wallowing in the ways of this world. "For whatever is born of God overcomes the world" (1 John 5:4). The superhero story is real. And it is being played out in every one of His children. Except, He is the hero and reveals Himself through us, and we are the beloved. God will complete His story in us and through us, as peculiar as that is. And this most gallant plot takes place, not just on the grand stages of history, in extraordinary events or a future kingdom, but within the simple everyday nuances of our lives. Though the action certainly emanates from within a royal home that He makes and accomplishes His unique plans. We can be confident of this work in us:

> Everyone who loves is born of God and knows God. . . . If we love one another, God abides in us, and His love is perfected in us. By this we know that we abide in Him and He in us, because He has given us of His Spirit. (1 John 4:7, 12–13)

Christ said, "In that day you will know that I am . . . in you" (John 14:20).

Christ builds that house within us now. Yet we

may not know in this life its magnificence or exactly how He will transform it with us, His holy body, into a collective dwelling for us all in or "from" heaven. Whether through bright sunshine or the dust of devastation, we squint to see the building and restoration. Maybe we get a glance at how both awe and awfulness bring the parts of our body together. A peek reveals how our foundation sets up further by our love for one another and as we rely on the head carpenter. I look ahead to being with all those I love, having all the profoundly troubling aspects and concerns of our lives resolved, and knowing completely. Paul relayed to us such great hope, "For now we see in a mirror dimly, but then face to face; now I know in part, but then I will know fully just as I also have been fully known" (1 Cor. 13:12). To the Romans, he said that "the sufferings of this present time are not worthy to be compared with the glory that is to be revealed to us" (Rom. 8:18). Yet even the current sufferings are something to rejoice over! Paul presents this attitude and with the reasons for it:

> We also exult in our tribulations, knowing that tribulation brings about perseverance; and perseverance, proven character; and proven character, hope; and hope does not disappoint, because the love of God has been poured out within our hearts through the Holy Spirit who was given to us. (Rom. 5:3–5)

God prepares and builds our more stately dwellings out of the nobility of hope sustained through endured sorrows. Hope appears to be an excellent mortar.

The author of the book of Hebrews wrote of those who, by faith, had obtained approval from God. But at this moment, one example stands out to me, the inspiring obedience of Abraham. But not just his offering of Isaac in faith, but his manner and hope in something else, seem particularly relevant.

"He went out, not knowing where he was going. By faith he lived as an alien in the land of promise . . . ; for he was looking for the city which has foundations, whose architect and builder is God" (Heb. 11:8–10). The promises made to Abraham, fellow heirs, Isaac and Jacob, and Sarah are also beautifully described. But the writer also poignantly reminds us:

> All these died in faith, without receiving the promises, but having seen them and having welcomed them from a distance, and having confessed that they were strangers and exiles on the earth . . . make it clear that they are seeking a country of their own. And indeed if they had been thinking of that country from which they went out, they would have had opportunity to return. But as it is, they desire a better *country*, that is, a heavenly one. Therefore God is not ashamed to be called their God; for He has prepared a

city for them. (Heb. 11:13–16)

The author also spoke of others who died by the sword and were even tortured (Heb. 11:35–37). The scriptures then explain, "And all these, having gained approval through their faith, did not receive what was promised, because God had provided something better for us, so that apart from us they would not be made perfect" (Heb. 11:39–40). There is something better for us as Jesus said,

> The glory which You have given Me I have given to them, that they may be one, just as We are one; I in them and You in Me, that they may be perfected in unity, so that the world may know that You sent Me, and loved them, even as You have loved Me. Father, I desire that they also, whom You have given Me, be with Me where I am, so that they may see My glory which You have given Me . . . . (John 17:22–24)

Somehow everything will be made complete. We will know fully and be perfected together in our magnificent home. All of us unite as one, our glorious body. Abraham finds that city built by God.

I look forward to personally meeting my grandfather, Shorty, though I believe I have met him already through my mom and experienced his love for me that way. I can imagine his baby blue eyes, like mine, and his leathery skin, tanned and dried through the West Texas sun. And his dirty khaki pants were caked with fine sands born from the erosion of distant mountains in past ages, only to arrive on him during the Dust Bowl of the Great Depression. I want to see my other grandfather, Milton, as well. I only know that after being gassed during the Meuse-Argonne battle, the bloodiest ever, of the First World War, he had spent over thirty years in hospitals and bed due to issues with his lungs until he died from complications of pneumonia when I was four. Who was he? Did he hold me as a baby? Did I smile and peer into the depths of his eyes? Did he know I would never know much about him in this mortal life, but someday I would? In my youth, I loved spending time with my grandmother Betty. She died when I was twenty. Despite her compromised mind, I believe she loved me. What a joy it will be to see her again and to know her, the soundly restored person, standing in that "fuller" light in which she spoke, and in which we all have hope.

We are all gloriously connected. Shorty loved, and he loved my mom. My mom loves me, and my dad loves me. And I love my kids. I love others because our Daddy loves me. He loves me so much through others, loves through me, and is so good. It's not the blood that connects us; it's the love. God is love. The only thing that can disconnect anybody is a lack of love. Yet God loves all of us; therefore, anyone can be part of the family. There are plenty of rooms. As Jesus said, "If it were not so, I would have told you."

CHAPTER SEVEN

The Final Leg

I will keep on wanting to explore places and continue to climb mountains. But those are not my destinations, not really where I am going. No longer will I moan the silence or grope blindly in the dark. I have searched high and low, and even the depths of this planet. There is, indeed, "a path which no bird of prey knows and the falcon's eye has not seen," but like Job, I asked, "Where can wisdom be found, and where is the place of understanding? Man does not know its value, nor is it found in the land of the living. The deep says, 'It is not in me'; and the sea says, 'It is not with me'" (Job 28: 7, 12–14). My problem was never Houston.

And that grand place where I can be part of something much greater than myself is not out there to be found somewhere. It is not in mountains, oceans, Alaska, or Norway. My hope is about a mansion being built within me.

As a child, I once ran downhill after an all-day walk up a mountain with my parents in Colorado. The hike had been too long and not all that interesting for a kid. I was excited at the thought of getting back to the campground. I was allowed to run ahead and did so as fast as I could. There was the feeling of lightness and almost a sense of flight as my body practically "fell" down the slope while my legs barely, more like magically, kept up to avoid my actual falling. While recently descending the last leg of a mountain climbing trip and trek in Uganda, I noticed the trail was becoming less muddy and the slope more gradual and even. The clouds had lightened, and the rain had stopped. All of this was a relief. The previous days were filled with long slogs through miles of muddy alpine bogs, down slick rocky canyons, and across unexpected rivers due to flash-flooding. It was mud, mud, and more mud, until now. I decided I could run — even in my wet boots and socks. I also very much wanted to go home. As I ran, I felt like I was gliding effortlessly through the bamboo trees and the jungle. The mist yielded to the warm sun. And in cadence with my steps, rays of light flickered in a strobe-like fashion through the canopy. When I saw better or gentler sections of the trail ahead, I quickened my stride. I flew. I hollered as I hurdled a downed tree across the path at full speed. On and on, I ran down the mountain joyfully. It was like I was reliving my childhood on that mountain long ago. I became young again. Finally, I rested and saw, to my surprise, my guides were there with me. They had run as well to keep up. At times I heard their laughter behind me, but I don't know if they enjoyed it as much as I did. I experienced the joy of my going home. And from what I had seen and heard, I suspect Jesus did too.

Made in the USA
Monee, IL
14 March 2024

55032133R00069